The Library of
NATIVE AMERICANS

The Illinois Confederacy

of Illinois, Missouri, Wisconsin, Iowa, and Oklahoma

Jennifer Lee

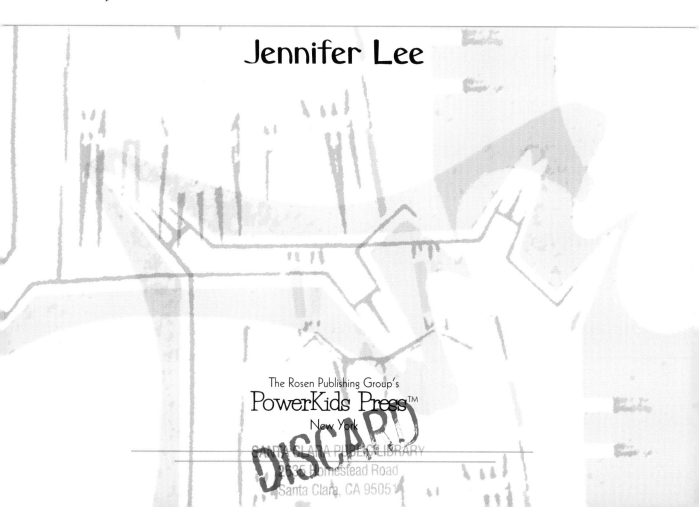

The Rosen Publishing Group's
PowerKids Press™
New York

Special thanks to Duane Esarey from the Dickson Mounds/Illinois State Museum
Also thanks to Annette Black, Administrative Assistant to the Peoria Tribe of Indians of Oklahoma

Published in 2005 by The Rosen Publishing Group, Inc.
29 East 21st Street, New York, NY 10010

Photo and Illustration Credits: Cover, Peabody Museum, Harvard University, Photo (T1231); p. 4 Mindy Liu; pp. 6, 39 Hulton Archive/Getty Images; p. 8 The Art Archive/National Anthropological Museum Mexico/Dagli Orti; p. 10 Library of Congress, Washington, D.C., USA/Bridgeman Art Library; pp. 12, 49 Smithsonian American Art Museum, Washington, D.C./Art Resource, NY; pp. 14, 22 Collection of the Illinois State Museum; p. 17 Peabody Museum, Harvard University, Photo (T1440); p. 19 Courtesy of the Illinois State Museum, Artist: Lynn E. Alden; p. 21 © Randy M. Ury/Corbis; p. 25 © Corbis; p. 28 Peabody Museum, Harvard University, Photo (T3009.2); p. 31 Tippecanoe County Historical Association, Lafayette, Indiana. Gift of Mrs. Cable Ball; p. 32 © Gianni Dagli Orti/Corbis; pp. 35, 43 © Bettman/Corbis; p. 36 Watercolor illustration by Andy Buttram. Courtesy of Dickson Mounds Museum, a branch of the Illinois State Museum; p. 41 Private Collection/Bridgeman Art Library; p. 44 © Indiana State Museum and Historic Sites; p. 47 Map and Geography Library, University of Illinois at Urbana-Champaign; pp. 50, 53 Peoria Tribe of Indians of Oklahoma, http://www.peoriatribe.com/; pp. 54–55 © Allen Russell/Index Stock Imagery, Inc.

Book Design: Erica Clendening
Book Layout, Illinois Confederacy Art, and Production: Mindy Liu
Contributing Editor: Kevin Somers

Library of Congress Cataloging-in-Publication Data

Lee, Jennifer, 1979–
   The Illinois Confederacy of Illinois, Missouri, Wisconsin, Iowa, and Oklahoma /
   Jennifer Lee.
      p. cm. — (The library of Native Americans)
   Includes index.
   ISBN 1-4042-2875-6 (lib. bdg.)
   1. Illinois Indians—History. 2. Illinois Indians—Social life and customs. I. Title. II.
   Series.

   E99.I2L44 2005
   977.004'97315—dc22

                                                          2004004046
Manufactured in the United States of America

Contents

Where the People of the Illinois Confederacy Lived

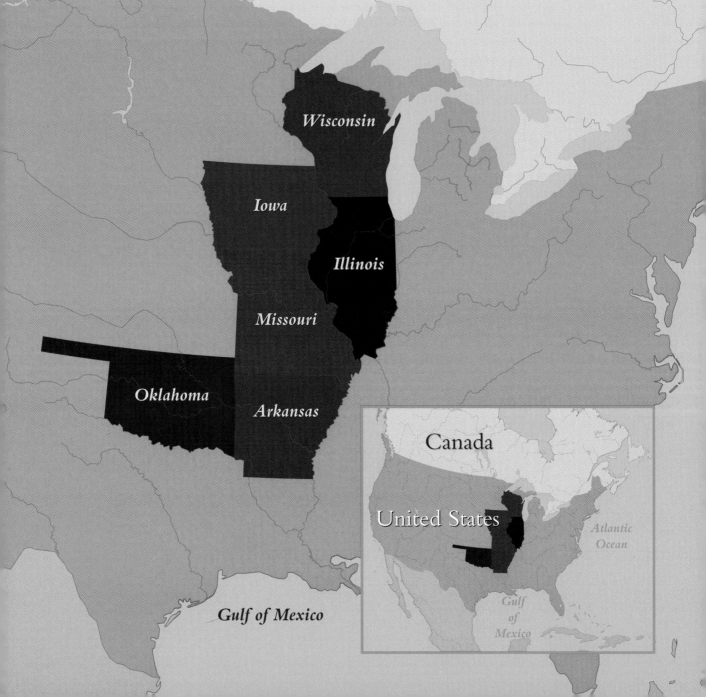

One

An Introduction to the Illinois Confederacy

Long ago, on the lands that were to become the United States of America, there was a variety of Native American peoples living in an area rich in natural resources. This area, which became Illinois and several surrounding states, was very appealing to its residents. Many disputes over the territory broke out between these peoples. Nations such as France, England, and later the United States also struggled against one another for control of this land. In the middle of these struggles were the native peoples of this region, now known as the Illinois Confederacy. These people battled against the wills of many, confronted war as an ongoing threat, and ultimately were forced out of their homeland.

The many cultures that made up the Illinois Confederacy shared numerous characteristics. The various tribes that made up the Confederacy called themselves the Inoca. However, the Ottawa nations who lived to the north called them the Ilinwe or, if plural, Ilinwek. These words are believed to have come from the Illinois word "irenweewa," which meant "he speaks in the ordinary way." French explorers learned the name Ilinwe from

This map shows the different places in which the Illinois have dwelled.

This illustration shows a meeting between men of the Illinois Confederacy and European newcomers.

the Ottawa. The French spelled the word Illinois. Both groups pronounced the word "ee-lin-way." The name of this territory, and later the state, comes from the French. The Illinois tribes shared a large area of land in the Mississippi River Valley. They moved in and out of many states covering a large territory. At different points in time, these nations lived in areas of Arkansas, Iowa, Wisconsin, and Missouri. Sometimes they spread beyond the borders of their land in order to hunt and fight.

Before the arrival of Europeans, the Illinois people produced practically all of the foods and other goods needed to maintain their way of life. However, they did participate in a trading network in order to get various goods from other nations. The Illinois traded with Great Lakes tribes and later with the French traders. Eventually, the Illinois grew to be dependent on this trade with the French who settled in their lands.

Two

Origins

Most scholars believe that sometime between 40,000 to 13,000 years ago, people from Asia came to North America by crossing a land bridge that stretched from Siberia to Alaska. During that time, the climate was much colder than it is now. Glaciers, or great sheets of ice, covered much of North America. These ancestors of the Native Americans slowly moved south. By 12,000 years ago, some of the people had reached the tip of South America. During the thousands of years that followed, these groups spread out, populating different regions of the Americas. Little is known about these very first Americans.

Some people think that long before the Europeans appeared on the American continents, the nations of the Illinois people all lived as one large nation. This nation may have moved and split apart into many different, smaller nations. It might have been beneficial to do this to avoid overhunting the areas in which they lived.

All of the nations of the Illinois Confederacy spoke a language in the Algonquian language family called Illinois-Miami. This was a language that could be understood by both the Illinois and the Miami peoples. The only major differences in the language were the way in which certain words were pronounced. The Illinois

The migration of people from Asia to North America over the land bridge, which has now become the Bering Strait, is portrayed in this painting from the National Anthropological Museum in Mexico.

spoke with different accents than the Miami. Many people think that the shared language of the Illinois nations is proof that they were originally one large group.

At the time Europeans arrived, many Illinois nations lived in the area. The Peoria and Moingwena occupied the northwestern part of the Mississippi River Valley region in an area that is eastern Iowa today. The Kaskaskia were living in the Illinois River Valley at this time. The Cahokia and Tamaroa lived in what is today western Illinois and eastern Missouri. Michigamea were living in what is now northeastern Arkansas. Many other nations of Illinois people were living in these areas at this time too. However, little is known about these smaller nations of the Illinois Confederacy, because many of them did not survive. As their populations

In 1796, French explorer General George-Victor Collot drew a sketch of a man from the Kaskaskia nation. The sketch was then used to create this engraving.

shrank due to war and disease, their surviving members were accepted into other nations of the Illinois Confederacy.

For the Illinois people, war was a fact of life. They often fought to defend or control their territory. Of the nations that the Illinois Confederacy found themselves at war with, their greatest enemies were the nations of the Iroquois Confederacy.

The Illinois also fought many other nations, such as the Chickasaw, Fox, Kickapoo, Mascouten, Missouri, Osage, Ottawa, Sioux, Winnebago, and Miami. Like the Illinois and the Iroquois people, the Miami were made up of many nations. These Miami nations shifted their loyalties as time went by. The Miami were not the only nations to do this. As situations changed, many nations were convinced, either through violence or other means, to fight for or against the nations that made up the Illinois Confederacy. Such nations moved back and forth between being enemies of the Illinois and being their allies.

All of these warring nations completely surrounded the Illinois. The constant presence of battles and wars on all sides of their territory took its toll on the Illinois people. Their population was greatly lowered. This led the Illinois people to hope for peace because it would give them the opportunity to rebuild their numbers. They never fully got this chance to rebuild. Few of the Illinois nations would survive.

Three

Culture and Daily Life

Although many different nations made up the Illinois Confederacy, life for the various communities was remarkably similar. From survival methods, such as hunting and farming, to spiritual ceremonies and cultural rituals, the Illinois peoples shared many of the same values and ways of life.

Clothing and Decoration

The Illinois traditionally wore clothing made from skins and furs from animals such as buffalo and deer. After their trading relationship with the French had changed their way of life, they began to wear clothes made from fabrics such as wool. The men often decorated their skin with tattoos in geometric patterns. The men, women, and children commonly painted their faces red.

The Illinois men and women wore a variety of ornaments. They wore necklaces and pendants that were traditionally made from items such as shells and catlinite, which is a soft, red stone. These items were later replaced with glass beads and metals such as silver and brass. Illinois men often wore headdresses made from feathers and necklaces decorated with woven animal hair and porcupine quills.

In 1830, American painter George Catlin made this portrait of a Peoria man. The man is dressed in fabrics and other items that were introduced to the Illinois by the Europeans.

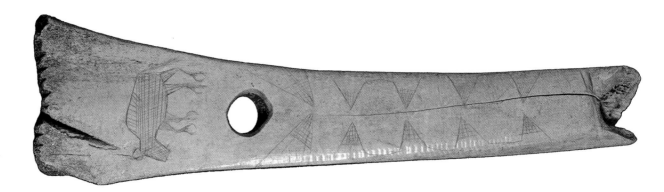

This is an arrow shaft wrench, which was used to straighten Illinois arrows. It was made from the rib of a bison.

Tools and Weapons

The Illinois made a wide variety of tools from different materials. Bones from animals such as deer, buffalo, or elk were used to make many different items. The Illinois used bones to make needles to sew. Wrenches used to straighten arrows were also made from bones. Shoulder blades from buffalo were made into garden tools. Ladles for cooking were made from the horns of buffalo. Spoons and hoes were made from mussel shells. Shells were also used as scraping tools.

Stone tools were made from rocks such as limestone, sandstone, and granitelike rocks. These stones were ground to make long chisels or axe heads. They were attached to handles to make hatchets or clubs. Granitelike stones were also used with slab-shaped stones called metates to grind corn.

The Illinois traditionally made containers from clay, bison hair, and plant fibers. Women gathered clay along the rivers and streams. They added crushed shells to the clay to make pots and other pottery items. The pots were jar-shaped vessels with thin necks that flared at the rims. Sometimes handles would be added. The pots were decorated and then baked in open fires. This made them durable and waterproof.

Illinois women made a variety of items out of cloth. The cloth was usually made from a yarn that was made of bison hair. Items such as leggings, scarves, and sacks for storing animal hides were made from this bison-hair cloth.

Illinois men used a number of weapons for war and for hunting. The bow and arrow were traditionally used for both war and hunting. Bows were made from wood. The arrows had heads made either from chipped stone or animal parts such as bone or antler. The Illinois also made spearheads from these same animal parts. Warriors were also known to carry knives, hatchets, and war clubs. They also used shields made from buffalo hides to defend themselves from arrow attacks. In later years, the Illinois men used flintlock guns that they got from French traders.

Illinois Arts

Illinois culture was rich with artistic traditions. For decoration or for ceremonial purposes, the Illinois created works of art from varied materials. Hide paintings were made by painting on the skins of buffalo, deer, elk, and other animals. The colors of paint were usually red, yellow, and black. Mats used for ceremonies or special events were also painted. Red, yellow, and gray dyes were used to decorate items such as belts and scarves. These dyes were also used on porcupine quills that would be put into headbands and moccasins. Wood carving was also a common artistic practice for the Illinois. Often, practical items such as bowls were carved into animal shapes.

Jewelry, such as this necklace, was made and worn by the Illinois as part of their artistic tradition. This necklace is believed to be from the Peoria Nation.

Recreation

The Illinois had a variety of recreational activities. They played sporting games and gambling games. Many Native American groups from this area played similar games.

Lacrosse was a sporting game that the Illinois, as well as many of their neighboring nations, played. In the game, two teams played against each other. The object of the game was to get a wooden ball

17

into a goal made of two upright poles. The poles were placed 10 paces apart in the middle of the field. To score, a team had to move the ball to one end of the field and return to pass the ball through the goal. Sinew-laced wooden rackets were used to carry, catch, and throw the ball. Teams were made up of men and women from different Illinois villages.

Men played a game of straws in which players placed bets. The game was played using a bundle of 200 1-foot-long straws. A pile of about 500 small seeds was also needed to play. The players used the seeds to register their guesses and to place bets. Then a player would randomly divide the bundle of straw in two. The straws in one of the bundles were then counted by sixes to determine the remainder. Any player who correctly guessed the remainder would claim the seeds for that round. The game went on until one player won all the seeds.

Housing and Transportation

The more permanent Illinois homes were their summer villages. They often preferred to build these village settlements along major rivers. In these villages, the Illinois built long, oval structures called longhouses. They were nearly 60 feet (18.3 meters) long and about 24 feet (7.2 m) wide. Longhouses were made with a framework of poles that were then covered with sheets of elm bark or mats. The Illinois people would weave dense mats from plants like cattails and similar stemmed marsh plants called bulrushes. Four to five hearths were put

This illustration of a longhouse by Lynn E. Alden gives us a look inside a typical home of an Illinois family.

in a row down the center of a longhouse. This provided one fire for every two families living in the house. Usually, these families were related. All of the extended families along the fathers' lines would live together in one longhouse.

The Illinois left these villages for six weeks during the summer to hunt. They built temporary camps to live in during summer hunting parties. They set up winter hunting camps where they would stay for half the year. The houses at the winter camps were called wigwams. Wigwams were smaller portable structures that were dome shaped. Wigwams had a framework of poles that were covered with mats.

Before Europeans brought horses to their lands, the Illinois people traveled on foot or by floating on rivers in dugout canoes. They made these boats from hollowed-out logs that were 40 to 50 feet (12.2 to 15.2 m) long. The French called these boats pirogues.

The Illinois used poles to move the dugout canoes through the water. These boats were valuable tools for moving heavy loads such as game animals and supplies for the moves between seasonal villages.

The Spanish started bringing horses to North America as early as the 1500s. The Apache began raiding Spanish horse-raising settlements by the 1650s. They soon began trading these horses with tribes living on the Great Plains. Horses reached the Illinois by 1711. At first, the Illinois only used these animals for work. Over time, the horse became an important means of transportation.

Horses, such as this mustang, were introduced to the Native Americans by the Spanish. Spanish settlers began breeding horses in North America in the 1600s.

This shell scraper is made from a freshwater mussel. Shells such as this were used to scrape corn off its cob.

Hunting and Fishing

Illinois men did the hunting and fishing. They hunted beaver, bear, buffalo, elk, deer, lynx, mountain lion, and turkey. Most animals were hunted by individuals or by small hunting parties. When hunting buffalo and deer, though, the Illinois men would form much larger hunting parties. During these hunts, the younger men surrounded the herd of animals. Then they would chase the herd toward the other hunters. These hunters were waiting with their weapons ready.

Gathering and Farming

The women of the Illinois nations spent most of their time working in the fields. In the spring, they planted beans, corn, pumpkin, squash, and watermelon. Europeans had brought watermelons to the Americas. Most of these crops were harvested in the fall. Illinois women also collected firewood and gathered wild foods such as pond lilies, pecans, and persimmons. These wild foods were preserved and stored to be eaten later.

Society

Traditionally, the people in Illinois society were equals. They had equal access to goods and resources. Tribal members had equal say in political matters. The chief was usually chosen because he was

23

good at keeping the peace among the nation's members. The decisions that affected the nation were decided on by all the members of the group. The chiefs had no more power than any other member of the nation in these political processes. However, this tradition was changed after contact with the Europeans. At this time, the leader was given more power and responsibility than he had had before.

Religion

The Illinois believed in one god above all others. This was Kitchesmanetoa, or the "spirit master of life." Kitchesmanetoa was believed to be the maker of all things. The Illinois believed that Kitchesmanetoa maintained life on Earth through the Sun and thunder. The Illinois honored the Sun and the thunder.

Manitous were the spirits that the Illinois men and women needed to connect with Kitchesmanetoa. Manitous took the forms of animals such as mountain lions, buffalo, deer, bear, and wolves. A warrior's animal manitou took the form of a bird.

The Illinois spiritual leaders were called shamans. They were men, although women sometimes held the status of shaman. The shaman began his or her training in childhood. Shamans learned how to be leaders and healers. Each shaman had a specific animal spirit that gave the shaman his or her knowledge. Young boys who behaved like girls were treated and raised as girls. These boys formed another category of religious leader, although they were not thought

This engraving from about 1850 shows a medicine man curing a patient. This work is based on a watercolor painting by American artist Seth Eastman.

to be as powerful as shamans. They were religious figures and were invited to rituals and meetings. They were often called upon when advice was needed.

Folklore

The Illinois had a rich oral tradition that included many folktales. These stories were important to the Illinois because they were an entertaining way to pass on their origins and beliefs to one another. The tales often explained why nature works the way it does and often had a moral to them. One of the most popular subjects of these folktales was Wisakatchekwa. He was a magical character who was responsible for the origin of the land and the people. Wisakatchekwa was also known for getting into all kinds of trouble.

How Wisakatchekwa Got into Trouble

Wisakatchekwa was traveling through the country and came across two old blind men who lived together by themselves. The men had a guide rope leading to the river where they got water. The old men agreed to let Wisakatchekwa stay with them in exchange for cooking their meals. He stayed for quite some time. One day, Wisakatchekwa asked them how two blind men hunted. The old men never told him. He grew tired of staying with them and decided to travel on. When he left, he changed the guide rope to go to the steep bank of the river. After he was gone, the old men, following their guide rope, fell into the river.

When Wisakatchekwa was far away, the old men decided to draw him back by smoking a pipe. This drew Wisakatchekwa back to the house. As he entered their home, the old men closed the door. They cornered Wisakatchekwa with spears and asked the scared Wisakatchekwa why he changed the guide rope to the water. He told them he changed that for himself and forgot to put it back. He begged them not to kill him and the old men let him go. He stayed with them a while longer.

One day while Wisakatchekwa was out hunting, the old men decided they wanted him to leave. When he returned, the old men told him they could get along without him if he was of a mind to travel. One of the old men finally told him how they caught so much game. The old man said, "I will tell you how we hunt, and you can do the same. Go to some big lake. There you will find all kinds of birds. Then you must use string to tie from your waist to each bird. Go from one bird to another tying them by their feet."

Wisakatchekwa did just what the old man had told him. When he attached himself to the birds with the string, they began to fly, raising him out of the water. They carried him for many days. He had nothing to cut the strings with. Finally, he asked for the strings to be broken, and they were. Then he began to fall. He fell into a hollow tree, and he was stuck there for several days. Finally, some people camping nearby heard him in the hollow tree and mistook him for a bear. When they cut the tree down to kill the bear, a frightened Wisakatchekwa came out.

The account of the Wisakatchekwa legend cited above is a shortened version based on the legend provided by George Washington Finley.

Rituals

Illinois culture was rich with ritual and celebration. There were rituals for spiritual events, war, and other important occasions. Birth, coming of age, marriage, and death were such occasions.

A calumet pipe was used to smoke tobacco. The Illinois used the pipe to strengthen friendships with other nations and to create peaceful relationships with strangers.

The Calumet Dance was a ceremony of major importance. It held great meaning socially, spiritually, and politically. Singers with good voices sang, while dancers took turns dancing with the calumet, or smoking pipe. Then a mock battle was performed between the head dancer, using the calumet to fight, and a warrior who used various weapons.

The birth of a child also carried with it certain rituals. Childbirth took place in a lodge separate from the family longhouse. When a child was born, the father cleaned the ashes from the fireplace. Then he lit a new fire before the mother returned with the child.

Young men of the nation went on dream quests, where they would pray for a vision of their spirit guardian. They went off by themselves and stayed alone without eating. Eventually, their spirit guardian would appear to them in a dream or vision. The spirit guardian was an animal that would guide and protect them. Once they found their spirit guardian, these young men were allowed to go on their first hunt. When a young boy killed his first animal, there would be a feast to celebrate his entry into manhood. Older men of the nation would honor his accomplishment.

Illinois girls who were maturing into young women also went off by themselves to fast. They waited for a vision that ensured well-being and spiritual gifts for the future.

Before a man could marry, he had to show his skill as a hunter. Once he did this, he brought presents to his future brother-in-law. If the gifts were good enough to please the family, the man proposed to his bride-to-be's father. If the man had shown his worth to the men of the woman's family, then the family allowed the couple to get married.

To the nations of the Illinois Confederacy, birds were a symbol of warfare. The men of the Illinois nations collected bird skins and kept them in colored reed mats. These men had all-night rituals in which the skins were displayed to gain the favor of the bird spirits. These skins would then be carried into battle.

The Illinois believed that there were many levels to the universe. They also believed that people were reincarnated, or reborn into a new body or form, when they died. When an Illinois person died, he or she was nicely dressed. Red paint was put around his or her head and hair. The men buried the men and the women buried the women. Families placed pots, food, bows, and other offerings in the graves to make sure that their loved ones would be allowed to enter the land of the dead. Then there would be ceremonies performed to honor the dead. Everyone would play the games that the dead person had liked while he or she was alive. The families of the dead would be given many gifts by other members of the nation. This was done as a sign of respect and to offer condolences to the dead people's families.

Painter George Winter became well known for historical accuracy in his work that captured the lives of Native Americans. He painted this burial scene during the late 1860s.

Four
Europeans and War

The Illinois fought with the nations to the north and south. Many of these battles may have been attempts to obtain the Illinois land. However, other battles were fought in response to attacks that the Illinois Confederacy had led. Battles to the west were fought in order to capture enemy people to use as slaves. The greatest threat to the Illinois came from the east in an area that is today New York State. This threat was the Iroquois Confederacy. The Iroquois were interested in the vast riches from the Illinois lands. Like the Illinois, the Iroquois were made up of many different nations. Throughout the seventeenth century, the five nations of the Iroquois Confederacy included the Cayuga, Mohawk, Oneida, Onondaga, and Seneca. By the eighteenth century, the Iroquois Confederacy had been joined by a sixth group, the Tuscarora Nations.

After this point, the Iroquois Confederacy was also known as the League of Six Nations. When these nations were united and worked together, they were incredibly strong. Whatever the reasons for the fighting, the intertribal wars were an ongoing threat to the peoples of the Illinois Confederacy. This threat would only grow worse after the arrival of the Europeans.

French artist J. Laroque created this illustration of an Iroquois warrior in 1796.

Early Contact with Europeans

In 1666, a group of Illinois traveled northward to a small French-Canadian trading post and mission located at Chequamegon Bay on the southwestern shore of Lake Superior. Here they met with a priest, Father Claude Allouez, the first of many Europeans to meet with the Illinois. Illinois traders made additional trips to Lake Superior during the next few years. They went to obtain goods such as guns, gunpowder, kettles, hatchets, and knives. Father Allouez and other missionaries wanted to teach the Illinois about Christianity. Father Jacques Marquette and other French missionaries wanted to set up a mission among the Illinois. In preparation, Marquette studied their language and learned what he could of their culture. Much of what we know of early Illinois culture comes from Marquette's studies.

Alliance with the French

The Peoria Nation of Illinois was living in a village at the mouth of the Des Moines River when they welcomed French visitors to the area in 1673. The Illinois and the French became allies and began trading.

At about this time, the British were buying furs from the Iroquois. The Iroquois attacked other nations to get control of trade routes and the lands where they could trap more animals. By the 1670s, the Iroquois and the Illinois were again at war.

34

Father Jacques Marquette was a priest who studied the language and culture of the Illinois people in the mid–1670s.

36   This illustration shows an Illinois man holding a flintlock gun. The French supplied the Illinois with these weapons to help them fight their Iroquois enemies.

The Iroquois were more powerful than the Illinois. The British had been supplying the Iroquois with guns and gunpowder for decades. This gave the Iroquois a huge advantage over their neighbors. The French, fearing that the Illinois Confederacy would be wiped out by the Iroquois, knew they had to arm their allies. They gave guns to the Illinois so that they would have a better chance of winning battles with the Iroquois.

At this time, the French convinced the Miami, who were fighting the Illinois, to make peace. If the Illinois people were free from battles with the Miami nations, they would be able to concentrate on their battles with the Iroquois.

Fort St. Louis

In 1682, a French explorer named René Robert Cavelier, Sieur de La Salle, built Fort St. Louis on the Illinois River. This site later became known as Starved Rock. This was at a time when the Illinois had been severely beaten by numerous enemies, including the Iroquois nations. The Illinois had spread outward to other territories. La Salle wanted to encourage the Illinois Confederacy to regroup in the Illinois territory to keep the Iroquois away. A fort would increase the Illinois nations' ability to protect and defend their territories.

By 1683, members of the Illinois Confederacy, plus the Mascouten, Shawnee, and Miami nations, had settled around Fort St. Louis. However, the Iroquois continued to raid their territories. In 1691, the French and the Illinois abandoned the Starved Rock area for lack of game and firewood. At this time, they relocated Fort St. Louis to Peoria, about 75 miles downstream.

During this same period, the Illinois sent war parties east to meet the Iroquois in battle. The Iroquois then began to plunder French canoes along the eastern trade routes. This forced the French to come to a truce with the Iroquois in order to continue their trade. The truce left the Illinois people without the protection of the French. This made Iroquois attacks even more difficult to withstand. However, this would not last for long.

Tired of having their trade routes interrupted, the French organized peace between the Iroquois and the nations allied with the French. This included the Illinois. The fighting between the Iroquois and Illinois ended in 1701.

LA SALLE

Designed and etched for Bancroft's History of the U. States.

René Robert Cavelier, Sieur de La Salle, is famous for making his way down the Mississippi River to the Gulf of Mexico. In 1682, he claimed the area in the name of France and named it Louisiana after King Louis XIV.

39

The Fox Wars

In 1712, several French allies, including the Ottawa and the Illinois, came to the aid of the French in a conflict with the Fox at Fort Detroit. The French and their Native American allies forced the Fox to withdraw. For decades after this, the Fox and the Illinois would be constantly at odds. In 1722, the Illinois at Starved Rock captured and killed a number of Fox prisoners. One of these prisoners was the nephew of a Fox chief. After this, the Fox sent a strong force into Illinois Country to attack them for what they had done. This raid cost the Illinois more than 100 lives.

In 1726, the angered French and Illinois set out with more than 500 warriors and soldiers to put an end to the Fox raids. However, the Fox learned of the coming attack and escaped.

For the next few years the French, the Illinois, and other Native American allies kept the Fox on the defensive. By 1729, the pressure on the Fox was too great. Their allies, the Kickapoo and the Mascouten, decided they would be safer and stronger fighting on the side of the French and the Illinois. This is when they left their alliance with the Fox.

This addition of allies strengthened the French and the Illinois as it weakened the Fox. The French saw their opportunity to conquer them. The French and their allies would have to attack the Fox before the Fox could go to the Iroquois Nations for protection. If the Fox

Artist Charles Bird King, famous for his portraits of Native Americans, created this illustration of a Fox chief. The illustration appeared in *The Indian Tribes of North America* by Thomas L. McKenney and James Hall.

41

were able to combine their forces with those of the Iroquois, then the Illinois and the French would not have a chance to win the battle. Luckily for the Illinois, the Fox were not able to reach their Iroquois allies. In 1730, the French, the Illinois, and their allies caught up with the Fox out in the prairies near Starved Rock and defeated them. This ended the Fox Wars.

The French and Indian War

Most of the Illinois nations did not like the British. The French had generally been considerate of Native American tribal customs. They respected and participated in ceremonial gift giving that was meant to show friendship and kindness. The British refused to participate in Native American customs. They mistook gift giving for bribery. For a time, some of the Illinois nations became friendly toward the British. However, most of the nations kept their loyalty to the French.

In 1754, the French and Indian War began. This was a war between the French and the British to decide who would take control of the Illinois Country. Native American nations fought on both sides of this conflict. The Illinois fought against the British. This put them on bad terms with the Indian nations who were British allies. Under French leadership and guidance, the Illinois had many successful raids against the British. The Peoria did not fight alongside the other members of the Illinois Confederacy at this point. They were busy with a renewed conflict with the Fox.

British Control of the Illinois Territory

The British won the French and Indian War and, in 1763, the Treaty of Paris gave the Illinois territories to the British. In an act of opposition, Chief Pontiac of the Ottawa Nation led a war party against the British in the same year. He was defeated. He stubbornly continued in his efforts to lead parties against the British. He was outnumbered and simply could not win.

The British began to watch closely over the Illinois people. By 1765, the British held tight control of the territory. This gave them the ability to prevent any further rebellions by the Illinois. The British tried repeatedly to persuade the Illinois Confederacy to unite with them, but the Illinois people would not.

Many of the Illinois nations chose to move away from the British settlement in the Illinois territory.

Chief Pontiac became famous for leading the Ottawa in uprisings against the British. These uprisings became known as Pontiac's Rebellion.

Most of the Illinois eventually returned. They needed to trade their furs and, since the French had been taken out of the picture, the British were the only people to sell to. The British did, however, keep the peace to protect the fur trade. If nations fought, it interrupted trade. Therefore, the British worked hard to keep the various groups from fighting.

The people of the Illinois Confederacy gave aid to the Americans during the American Revolutionary War. Many other Native American groups sided with the British. This painting shows a group of Native American British allies being captured by American soldiers.

In 1777, the Kaskaskia were in Spanish territory around Lake Genevieve in modern-day Missouri. Attacks from the Sauk at this time convinced the Kaskaskia that they would be stronger if they regrouped with other nearby Illinois nations. They united with the peoples of the Peoria and the Cahokia for strength.

The Illinois Aid the American Colonies

When the American colonies rose up against British rule, the loyalties of Native American nations were divided. By 1778, the Cherokee and the Chickasaw had joined the British. Many of the Illinois nations helped the American colonies. The Illinois had been allies with the French for a very long time, and the French were aiding the Americans too. The Illinois, along with the Kickapoo and Miami nations, aided the American armies by supplying them with food and acting as scouts.

Their participation in the war would bring the Illinois to the brink of extinction. The Iroquois and Fox wars, followed by the French and Indian War, had left the Illinois weak and few in number. By the end of the American Revolutionary War, the Illinois population was a fraction of what it had been less than two centuries earlier. There were less than 100 members left in each remaining nation.

Surviving the Wars

By the late 1700s, the Michigamea and the Tamaroa joined the Kaskaskia Nation. The Kaskaskia had remained in Illinois Country. They had been largely depleted by constant battles. By 1764, alcohol, disease, and war had largely crushed the Kaskaskia. Many nations of the Illinois met fates similar to that of the Kaskaskia.

The Cahokia and Kaskaskia sought rest, peace, and a place to rebuild their numbers. This led them to exchange their land in Illinois for two reservations. On August 13, 1803, the United States assigned them one reservation of 350 acres (141.64 hectares). They were allowed to choose a second area of 640 acres (259 ha). They chose a plot of land in Jackson County, Illinois. They hoped that these reservations would allow them to live quietly and undisturbed. They would not experience massive wars as they had before, but they would not be able to keep the Jackson County reservation for long. Soon after the United States granted them the Jackson County land, European immigrants moved in. This forced the Native Americans out of Jackson County.

On September 25, 1818, the Peoria signed a treaty with the United States. This treaty granted the Peoria 640 acres (259 ha) that included their village at Blackwater River, Missouri.

Many of the Illinois' neighbors faced similar hardships at this time. Peoples such as the Weas and the Piankashaw, both subtribes

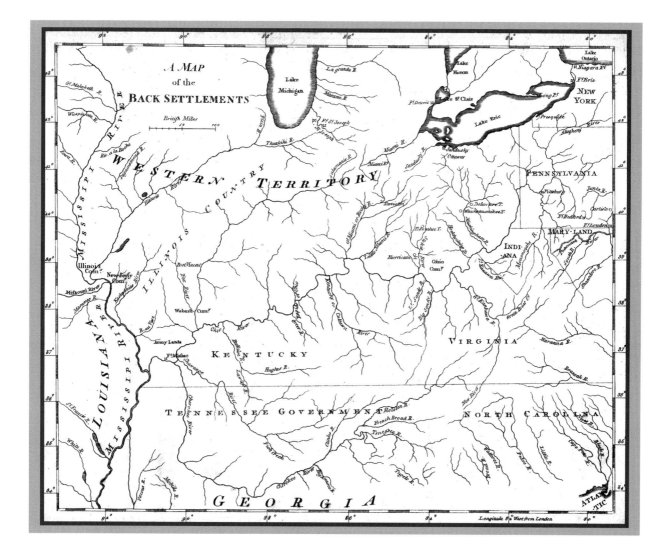

This map, A Map of the Back Settlements, was drafted by John Stockdale. The map was made in 1794, a time of great hardship for the native peoples of the Illinois Country.

of the Miami Nation, were having difficulties holding on to their native lands. In October 1818, the Weas had to give up most of their lands in Indiana, Ohio, and Illinois. Their remaining lands in Indiana would be given up in a treaty of 1820. Having given up their lands, the remaining Wea moved to Arkansas and Missouri. They joined the tribal members, along with the Piankashaw, who had relocated there earlier.

In a treaty signed on October 29, 1832, the Wea, along with the Piankashaws, were granted 250 sections of land next to the Peoria and Kaskaskia Reserve in what is today Miami County, Kansas.

There were a few other Illinois survivors by the time peace had come. These few Illinois survivors joined with the Peoria to become members of their nation. These survivors included members of nations such as the Kaskaskia. In 1854, the United States recognized the surviving Illinois members, along with their neighbors, the Wea and Piankashaw, as the Peoria Tribe of Indians of Oklahoma. By 1865, there were only 220 remaining members of the nation that had once been the plentiful Illinois.

George Catlin painted this portrait of a Peoria chief in 1830. By the time this portrait was painted, the Peoria had been removed from their homeland.

Five

The Illinois Today

Today, the Peoria Tribe of Indians of Oklahoma is all that remains of the Illinois Confederacy, as well as of the Wea and the Piankashaw nations. Now, they have their headquarters in Miami, Oklahoma. They have survived hundreds of years of war and oppression.

The Peoria of Miami, Oklahoma, have developed a tribal emblem that represents their people. It has four arrows across each other, and each one represents a nation that makes up the Peoria. The green arrow is for the Kaskaskia, and it represents the grass and the trees. The red arrow is for the Peoria, and it represents the Sun. The turquoise arrow is for the Piankashaws, and it represents the soil. The blue arrow is for the Weas, and it represents the water. Underneath all of these arrows lies an arrowhead that represents the ability of these nations to work together with the common goal of preserving customs and culture today.

The Peoria have worked together to accomplish a great deal. They have tribal systems and services to help their members. Many of the services that the tribal government provides are the same ones that a state in the union gives its residents. This includes groups that provide housing and groups that maintain the roads.

These women are participating in the Grand Entry at a powwow. The Grand Entry starts off the powwow, and any dancer in traditional dress may enter.

Other tribal programs make sure that children are well cared for. Others work with the U.S. Environmental Protection Agency to help protect the environment. Nutrition programs, election committees, social services, education committees, and scholarships are among the services provided. The Federal Bureau of Indian Affairs helps the individual tribes. It develops laws and policies to help resolve inter-tribal disputes, among other things.

One of the large projects underway is an attempt to have the ownership of cultural objects and remains returned to the Peoria. In 1990, a law was passed that makes sure that the property rights for such items are protected. It also allows tribal members to be buried on tribal lands.

Another investment that the tribal council has undertaken is the Peoria Ridge Golf Course. Golf tournaments, as well as events for children and elders, are held here. It has become a tourist attraction and draws people from places as far away as Arkansas, Kansas, and Missouri. The golf course helps to add to the tribe's income.

The tribe also holds a Christmas party at the Ottawa/Peoria Culture Center. Tribe members within 90 miles (233 kilometers) of Miami, Oklahoma, are invited. It is sponsored by the profits from the sale of Peoria bottled water. The tribal council gives each child a toy and a gift bag.

A bead class is held every week at the Peoria Tribal Office. People are taught how to make native jewelry. For each piece they make, they make a piece of jewelry for the tribal store. This money that the tribal store makes goes back to the beading class.

The committees for culture and language often work with the Oklahoma Miami tribe committee. These groups work to keep tribal culture alive and to organize festivals and events. They hold stomp dances and powwows. At a Peoria Stomp Dance, dancing is done in a counterclockwise direction. At the center of the dance circle are the drummer and singers. The women dancers wear special leggings fitted with turtle shells or aluminum cans filled with pebbles. The sounds of the shells and cans, along with the drum, form the rhythm of the dance. Male dancers do not wear any special clothing.

Powwows are traditional celebrations that bring people and tribes together. Both men and women dance. There are rules of courtesy

Peoria Ridge Golf Course is a championship course famous for attracting golfers from all over. Golf memberships, tournaments, and outings help earn income for the tribe's community.

and local traditions that are followed at powwows. The direction of dancing varies among tribal nations and events. At the Peoria pow-wow, dancing is done in a clockwise direction. Honor dances and blanket dances are a part of most powwows. During these dances, gifts are presented to the person or group being honored. Those being honored are not to pick up the gifts. Someone else picks up the gifts and later gives them to those being honored. In addition to the dances at the powwow, songs are sung. Special songs include those

sung during the grand entry, flag songs, veterans songs, memorials, and prayers.

The Peoria work together to help their people thrive and to maintain and restore their rich heritage. Although much of their language and culture has been lost, various projects and groups work to reclaim important cultural items and revive as much of their language and culture as possible. Today, through the lives of the people from the Peoria Tribe of Indians of Oklahoma, the spirit of the Illinois lives on.

Having been removed from their homelands in what was once Illinois Country, the Peoria Tribe now live in Oklahoma.

Timeline

13,000 to 40,000 years ago	Ancient ancestors of the Native Americans travel from Asia to North America.
1666	Illinois travel north to have first face-to-face contact with French missionary Father Claude Allouez.
1670s	Illinois and Iroquois wage war.
1673	The French are welcomed into the Illinois region.
1682	René Robert Cavelier, Sieur de La Salle, builds Fort St. Louis at Starved Rock in order to assist the Illinois Confederacy's struggles.
1683	Members of the Illinois Confederacy, plus the Mascouten, Shawnee, and Miami nations, settle around Fort St. Louis.
1691	The Illinois abandon Fort St. Louis.

1701	The French arrange a peace agreement between the Iroquois Nation and the Illinois Confederacy.
1712	The Illinois come to the aid of the French in a conflict with the Fox at Fort Detroit.
1729	The Kickapoo and Mascouten leave the alliance with the Fox to join sides with the Illinois and the French.
1730	The French and the Illinois catch the Fox on the prairies near Starved Rock and defeat them, ending the Fox Wars.
1754	The French and Indian War begins.
1763	Treaty of Paris grants the Illinois land to the British.
1778	The Cherokee and Chickasaw aid the British, while many Illinois tribes aid the American colonies.
1803	The Illinois are granted land in Jackson County, Illinois.
1818	Treaty with United States grants the Peoria a large territory in Missouri.

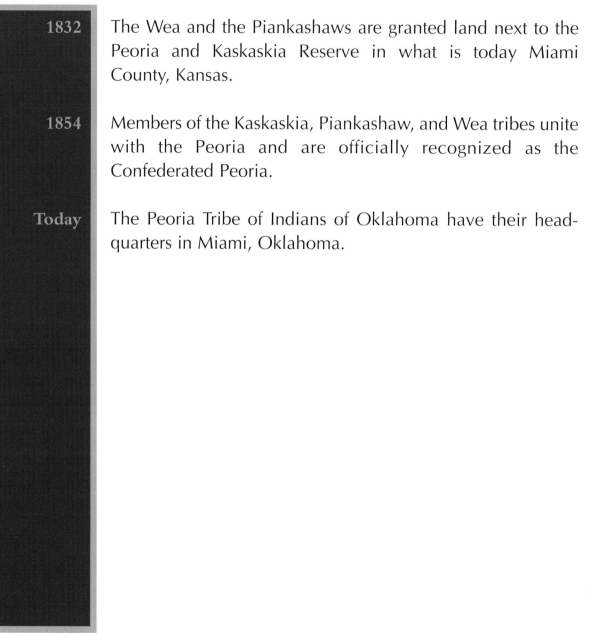

1832   The Wea and the Piankashaws are granted land next to the Peoria and Kaskaskia Reserve in what is today Miami County, Kansas.

1854   Members of the Kaskaskia, Piankashaw, and Wea tribes unite with the Peoria and are officially recognized as the Confederated Peoria.

Today   The Peoria Tribe of Indians of Oklahoma have their headquarters in Miami, Oklahoma.

Glossary

accents (AK-sentz) The ways you pronounce words.

Algonquian (al-GON-kwee-uhn) A family of American Indian languages. Not all speakers of Algonquian languages could understand each other, although some of the languages had words in common.

alliance (uh-LY-ens) An agreement between two or more groups in order to achieve a common goal.

category (KAT-uh-gor-ee) A class or group of things that has something in common.

cattails (KAT-taylz) A tall, thin plant with long, brown, furry pods at the top and narrow leaves.

condolences (kuhn-DOH-luhn-suhz) An expression of sympathy for a person who is upset because a friend or relative died.

confederacy (kuhn-FEH-duh-ruh-see) A group of people or nations that are united and that share the same beliefs.

customs (KUHS-tuhmz) The traditions in a culture.

disputes (dis-PYOOTS) Disagreements.

flintlock (FLINT-lok) A gun fitted with a flint hammer.

headdress (HED-dress) A covering, often decorative, for the head.

hearth (HARTH) A pit used for fires.

intertribal wars (IN-tur-TRY-buhl WARZ) Wars fought between two or more nations.

longhouse (LONG-hows) A dwelling made of wood, straw mats, or bark. As the name suggests, it is long in shape.

nation (NAY-shun) A group of people who share the same beliefs and follow the same laws.

oppression (oh-PRE-shun) The act of treating people in a cruel, unjust, and hard way.

persimmon (pur-SI-muhn) An orange-red fruit that is shaped like a plum and is sweet and soft when ripe.

reservation (rez-ur-VAY-shuhn) An area of land set aside by the government for a special purpose, as in a tribal reservation.

ritual (RICH-oo-uhl) A set of actions that is always performed in the same way as part of a religious ceremony or social custom.

scholarships (SKOL-ur-ships) A grant or prize that pays for you to go to college or to follow a course of study.

shamans (SHAH-muhnz) Spiritual leaders who act as healers.

sinew (SIN-yoo) A strong fiber or band of tissue that connects a muscle to a bone; a tendon.

truce (TROOSS) A temporary agreement to stop fighting.

Resources

BOOKS

Bauxar, J. Joseph. "History of the Illinois Area." In *Handbook of North American Indians*, Vol. 15. Washington, D.C.: Smithsonian Institution, 1978.

Bragdon, Kathleen J. *The Columbia Guide to American Indians of the Northeast.* New York: Columbia University Press, 2002.

Callender, Charles. "Illinois." In *Handbook of North American Indians*, Vol. 15. Washington, D.C.: Smithsonian Institution, 1978.

Milner, George R. *The Cahokia Chiefdom.* Washington, D.C.: Smithsonian Institution Press, 1998.

Temple, Wayne. *Indian Villages of the Illinois Country.* Springfield, IL: Illinois State Museum, 1966.

Valley, Dorris, and Mary M. Lembcke. *The Peorias: A History of the Peoria Tribe of Oklahoma.* Miami, OK: The Peoria Indian Tribe of Oklahoma, 1991.

MUSEUMS

Dickson Mounds/Illinois State Museum
10956 N. Dickson Mounds Road
Lewiston, Il 61542
(309) 547-3721
website: http://www.museum.state.il.us/ismsites/dickson/
homepage.htm

WEB SITES

Due to the changing nature of Internet links, PowerKids Press has developed an online list of Web sites related to the subject of this book. This site is updated regularly. Please use this link to access the list:

www.powerkidslinks.com/lna/illinoisconfederacy

Index

Index

K

Kaskaskia, 10, 45–46, 48, 51
Kickapoo, 11, 40, 45
Kitchesmanetoa, 24

L

language, 9–10, 34, 53, 55
League of Six Nations, 33
longhouses, 18

M

manitous, 24
Marquette, Father Jacques, 34
Mascouten, 11, 37, 40
Miami, 9–11, 37, 45, 48, 51–53
Michigamea, 10, 46
Mississippi River Valley, 7, 10
Missouri, 7, 10–11, 45–46, 48, 52
Moingwena, 10

O

ornaments, 13
Osage, 11
Ottawa, 5, 11, 40, 43, 52

P

Peoria, 10, 34, 38, 42, 45–46, 48
Peoria Tribe of Indians of Oklahoma,
    48, 51–52, 55
Piankashaws, 48, 51

R

rituals, 13, 26, 28–30

S

shamans, 24, 26
Shawnee, 37
Sioux, 11
spirit guardian, 29
Starved Rock, 37, 38, 40, 42

T

Tamaroa, 10, 46
Treaty of Paris, 43
tribal emblem, 51

W

Wea, 46, 48, 51
wigwams, 20
Winnebago, 11
Wisakatchekwa, 26